00175111

KT-197-667

DIABETES

Jo Whelan

HODDER
Wayland

an imprint of Hodder Children's Books

Published in Great Britain in 2002 by Hodder Wayland, an imprint of Hodder Children's Books

This book was produced for White-Thomson Publishing Ltd by Ruth Nason.

Design: Carole Binding
Picture research: Glass Onion Pictures

The right of Jo Whelan to be identified as the author of this work has been asserted by her in accordance with the Copyright, Designs and Patents Act 1988.

British Library Cataloguing in Publication Data
Whelan, Jo
   Diabetes. - (Health Issues)
   1. Diabetes - Juvenile literature
   I. Title II. Nason, Ruth
   616.4'62

ISBN 0 7502 3940 9

Printed in Hong Kong

Hodder Children's Books
A division of Hodder Headline Limited
338 Euston Road, London NW1 3BH

Acknowledgements
The author and publishers thank the following for their permission to reproduce photographs and illustrations: Carole Binding: pages 34, 36, 37, 38, 43b; Camera Press: page 8 (Richard Open); Martyn Chillmaid: pages 10, 14, 15, 18, 23, 26, 27, 39b, 48, 54, 59t, 59b; Corbis Images: pages 5 (O'Brien Productions), 40r (Hulton-Deutsch Collection); Angela Hampton Family Life Picture Library: pages 4, 12, 19, 50t; Imaging Body: page 58; Impact: pages 11 (Bruce Stephens), 40l (Bruce Stephens, 53 (John Cole), 56b (Bruce Stephens); Mediscan: cover and pages 1 and 55; Photofusion: pages 30 (Tina Gue), 46 (Crispin Hughes); Popperfoto/Reuters: pages 13, 56t; Science Photo Library: pages 6 (BSIP VEM), 7 (Damien Lovegrove), 9 (Catherine Pouedras/Eurelios), 21 (Dr L. Orci/University of Geneva), 22 (Saturn Stills), 25t (Will and Deni McIntyre), 25b (Saturn Stills), 29 (Klaus Guldbrandsen), 42 (Hattie Young), 43t (Simon Fraser), 44 (C C Studio), 45 (Manfred Rage), 47 (Dr H. C. Robinson), 49 (Alfred Pasieka); Topham Picturepoint: page 52; Wayland Picture Library: pages 20, 28, 39t, 41, 51. The quotation on page 58 is from *Diabetes for Beginners (Type 1)*, published by Diabetes UK, London, 2000.

Note: Photographs illustrating the case studies in this book were posed by models.

Contents

Introduction
A growing concern

Diabetes (or diabetes mellitus, to use its full name) is a common condition that affects all age groups, from toddlers to the elderly. The number of cases is rising around the world as more and more people become overweight through a combination of over-eating and lack of exercise. There also seems to be an increase in the number of children getting diabetes. The disease is a major cause of ill-health and costs millions of pounds in health services and lost working time.

There are two types of diabetes (type 1 and type 2), each with its own distinctive pattern. What unites them is the body's inability to use glucose properly. Glucose is the simplest form of sugar, and is the end product of the starchy and sugary foods (carbohydrates) that we eat. It is normally absorbed by the body's cells for use as fuel, but in people with diabetes this does not happen. Glucose builds up in the blood, causing both short-term symptoms and longer-term complications.

'Type 2 diabetes is nearing epidemic proportions, due to an increased number of older Americans, and a greater prevalence of obesity and sedentary lifestyles.' (American Diabetic Association)

If untreated, diabetes can cause serious illness and death. However, both types are fully treatable, allowing those affected to lead normal lives. There is no cure as yet, so treatment has to be taken for life. To reduce the risk of serious health problems in the future, people with diabetes also need to eat a healthy diet, take regular exercise and give up smoking – in fact the same health advice that applies to everyone.

About this book

The aim of this book is to give general information about diabetes and the way it affects people's lives. This is not meant to be a handbook providing health advice for people with diabetes. For that kind of advice, you should consult your doctor or diabetes nurse, or refer to a publication written specifically for people with diabetes.

Everyday life
Diabetes can affect people of all ages, but with proper treatment they can lead normal, active lives.

Chapter 1 gives basic facts and figures about diabetes, and Chapter 2 looks at the short-term symptoms caused by high blood glucose. In Chapter 3 we describe how diabetes is treated, either with insulin injections or with tablets. Diet is the other important aspect of treatment, and this is discussed in Chapter 4. Chapter 5 looks at the long-term complications that can arise from diabetes over the years, and Chapter 6 focuses on how diabetes affects people in everyday life. On pages 60-62 you will find a glossary explaining some of the less familiar words used in the book and a list of useful sources of information.

1 What is diabetes?
High levels of blood glucose

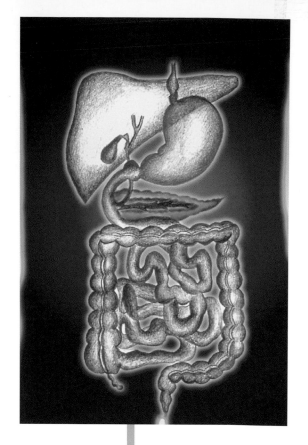

Diabetes is a disease in which the body is unable to use glucose properly. All the sugary and starchy foods we eat are broken down into glucose as we digest them; glucose is actually a simplified form of sugar. After digestion the glucose is carried round the body in the bloodstream and taken in by individual cells to provide them with the fuel they need to function. Inside the cell the glucose is 'burnt' in a series of chemical reactions. This releases energy, just as burning petrol in a car engine releases energy to drive the wheels.

The level of glucose in the blood is carefully controlled to stop it going too high or too low. When we eat, a hormone called insulin is released from the pancreas, an organ that sits behind the stomach. Insulin controls the way in which glucose is used and stored:

- ⊛ It helps cells to take glucose in.
- ⊛ It tells the liver to store glucose, ready to release it when levels drop again.

In people with diabetes this system does not work properly, either because they can't make insulin or because their cells don't react to it. Glucose levels in their blood become too high, and their cells may not be able to get the fuel they need.

The pancreas

In this illustration of the human digestive system, the pancreas is highlighted in blue. The liver is top left and the stomach top right. The small and large intestine are at the bottom.

How common is diabetes?

In the UK

- About 4 per cent of people have diabetes.

- 1.4 million people have been diagnosed; around one million others have it without realizing.

- Diabetes affects at least 20,000 people under the age of 20.

If not treated, diabetes causes serious problems and sometimes death. The symptoms of diabetes are discussed in Chapter 2, and the long-term complications in Chapter 5.

There are two forms of diabetes, known as type 1 and type 2.

Type 1 diabetes

Type 1 accounts for only 10-25 per cent of diabetes cases, but is probably better known than type 2. People with type 1 diabetes have lost the ability to make insulin and depend on insulin injections to survive. Because of this, it is also known as insulin-dependent diabetes.

Type 1 diabetes

People with type 1 diabetes can only survive if they inject insulin regularly.

Who gets it, and what are the causes?

Type 1 diabetes usually starts under the age of 30, and often in childhood or the teenage years. Children as young as 18 months can be affected. About 1 child in 600 has the condition. It seems to be becoming more common, especially in young children, but no one knows why.

Type 1 diabetes happens when the insulin-producing cells in the pancreas (the B cells) are destroyed by a person's own immune system. Human blood and tissues contain specialized cells – known collectively as white cells – which recognize and destroy invaders such as bacteria and viruses. In some people, for some reason, these cells mistake the pancreatic B cells for foreign invaders and begin to attack them. (Diseases where the body attacks itself in this way are called autoimmune diseases.) Over a period of time the B cells are wiped out until there are no more left to produce insulin. Symptoms develop quickly once insulin production falls (see Chapter 2), and it is soon obvious that the person is ill.

Children

More young children are developing type 1 diabetes than in the past, but the peak age of onset of the disease is around 12.

Type 1 diabetes is not inherited, but scientists think that some people's genetic make-up makes them more susceptible to it. In contrast to type 2 diabetes, being overweight does not increase the risk. Neither type of diabetes is caused by eating too much sugar.

Diabetes insipidus

Diabetes insipidus is a rare condition in which large amounts of pale, watery urine are passed. It is caused by a fault in the body's water-balancing system, and has nothing to do with diabetes mellitus (the subject of this book).

Type 2 diabetes

Type 2 diabetes is much more common than type 1, accounting for 75-90 per cent of cases. People with type 2 can still make insulin, but they either make too little or their bodies have become insensitive to it. This form of the disease used to be called non-insulin-dependent diabetes, but the term is misleading because some people with type 2 *do* need insulin injections.

Some people wrongly refer to type 2 as 'mild diabetes'. Although the symptoms can be mild, years of high blood glucose often cause serious damage leading to disability and early death. Getting treatment makes this much less likely.

Who gets it, and what are the causes?

Type 2 diabetes nearly always starts in adulthood, usually in those over 40. However, it is becoming commoner in people in their thirties, and in children and young people who are overweight. We do not know what causes it, but about 80 per cent of people with type 2 diabetes are overweight. Genetic make-up also plays a part: type 2 is not directly inherited, but people with a close relative who has the disease are at higher risk of getting it themselves. Some ethnic groups are also at higher risk, particularly when they take up the diet and lifestyle common in the rich countries of the developed world.

At risk
Being overweight increases a person's risk of developing type 2 diabetes.

The symptoms of type 2 diabetes develop slowly, and many people have it for several years before they realize that anything is wrong. About half show signs of long-term complications (see Chapter 5) by the time they are diagnosed. Diabetes specialists say everyone should be tested for diabetes if they are over 40 and have any high risk factors. These are:

- being overweight
- having a close relative with diabetes
- having African-Caribbean, African-American, Native American, Pacific Island or South Asian ethnic origin
- having a history of diabetes in pregnancy or giving birth to a baby over 4 kilos (9 lbs).

Type 2 diabetes and young people

Increasing numbers of young people are being diagnosed with type 2 diabetes. Until a few years ago this was extremely rare, but doctors in the USA say that anywhere between 8 and 45 per cent of new diabetes cases in under-18s are now type 2. A similar trend is emerging in Britain. Most cases of type 2 in young people occur in the 12-16 age group, and the great majority of those affected are overweight. Most of them also have a close relative with type 2 – although sometimes this is only recognized after the child's diabetes has been confirmed.

The importance of diet
Burgers and chips are high-fat foods. A diet with too much fat is not healthy.

The symptoms of type 2 in young people are usually much milder than those of type 1 (see Chapter 2), and may not be noticeable at all. Diabetes is diagnosed after blood and urine tests.

The increase in type 2 diabetes among young people is thought to be due to rising levels of obesity. Obesity is caused by eating too many calories and taking too little exercise. If obesity continues to rise at the current rate, doctors expect that type 2 diabetes will start to be seen in even younger children. Children diagnosed with the condition will probably have to take medication for the rest of their lives.

Indoor play

Too much time spent on computer games or TV can stop young people getting the exercise they need.

Body fat

The more fat someone carries on their body, the higher their risk of developing type 2 diabetes. A fat person needs to make more insulin than a thin person to produce the same effect. If their pancreas has a high insulin output it will cope with the extra demand. If the pancreas is weak, it will not be able to make enough, and the person will get diabetes. That is why losing weight is important for bringing type 2 diabetes under control. However, body fat is not the whole story. About 20 per cent of those affected by type 2 are not overweight.

Diabetes and pregnancy

Some women develop a temporary form of diabetes while they are pregnant. This is called gestational diabetes, and usually disappears after the baby is born. However, affected women may have a greater chance of developing type 2 diabetes later in life. Babies whose mothers have diabetes are often larger than average, because they receive extra glucose from the mother's blood. The baby becomes used to producing large amounts of insulin in response, and this can lead to temporary but potentially serious problems with low blood glucose levels after birth. These babies are also thought to be at greater risk of diabetes as adults.

Diabetes around the world

The World Health Organization estimates that diabetes affects about 140 million people worldwide. Within 25 years, the figure is expected to more than double to reach 300 million, with the largest increase happening in the developing world. Most of the new cases will be type 2. Many ethnic groups from developing countries seem especially vulnerable to diabetes when they take on the lifestyle typical of the Western world – a high-calorie diet rich in sugar and fat, and reduced levels of physical activity. For example, people with ethnic origins in Africa, South Asia or the Pacific Islands are significantly more likely to get type 2 diabetes than white people (except for whites of Hispanic origin, who also have a high incidence). Some scientists think the reason may be genetic: so-called 'thrifty genes', which allow survival when food is scarce, may increase the risk of obesity and diabetes from a Western-type diet.

Pregnancy
Gestational diabetes may occur during pregnancy. At every antenatal check-up, women have their urine tested for sugar.

Tonga – a Pacific Island kingdom

In Tonga, large body size was traditionally a sign of high status. King Taufa'ahau Topou IV was in the 'Guinness Book of Records' as the world's heaviest monarch – he weighed 460 lbs (33 stone, or 209 kilos). But Tonga, like other countries in the Pacific, has seen an epidemic of diabetes in the last 20 years. The problem is so bad that the government has set up a special programme to tackle it.

For centuries, fruit, vegetables and fish were the mainstays of the Tongan diet. But this changed as people came into contact with the Western way of life. Bread, sugary drinks and fatty tinned meats replaced traditional favourites. New ways of living meant people took less exercise. The end result was widespread obesity and some of the highest rates of diabetes in the world. Lack of awareness meant many people went untreated, leading to a high incidence of serious complications like blindness, kidney failure and amputation.

Now Tongans are being encouraged to change their lifestyle. The aim is to reduce levels of obesity, improve the national diet and encourage regular exercise. The king has lost weight and there is a national slimming competition. Exercise classes and organized walks are available. Slowly, people are beginning to rediscover some of the benefits of their traditional way of life.

Sign of status

King Taufa'ahau Topou IV in 1972, before the Tongans had recognized the dangers of being overweight.

2 Symptoms of diabetes
Tell-tale signs

The immediate symptoms of diabetes occur when blood glucose levels are high. They disappear once the person receives treatment and their condition is brought under control, but they can return if control begins to slip. In type 2 diabetes the symptoms are sometimes quite mild and develop slowly, making them hard to spot. In type 1 they are unmistakable.

Diabetes can also cause long-term complications which build up over the years. These are discussed in Chapter 5.

A tiring cycle
Two of the most obvious symptoms of the onset of diabetes are a need to urinate unusually often and severe thirst. Both can make it difficult to sleep.

Excessive urination

Excessive urination is one of the key symptoms of diabetes. When the level of glucose in the blood rises above a certain point, glucose is filtered out by the kidneys and appears in the urine. In the kidneys the glucose draws extra water into the urine, and so the amount produced rises. Someone with uncontrolled type 1 diabetes may pass up to five times the normal amount of urine – as much as 7.5 litres (13 pints) a day. Up to a kilo of glucose can be lost in the urine daily. With type 2 diabetes the effect is usually less extreme.

'I was going to the toilet every hour. The more I peed, the more thirsty I got. I just wanted to drink all the time.'
(Dave, 16)

Diabetes in history

The full name for diabetes is diabetes mellitus, a term derived from a Greek word for 'flowing through' and the Latin word for 'sweet'. A condition involving large amounts of sweet urine was first described around 2000 years ago. To test for diabetes, the doctor would taste the patient's urine to see if it contained sugar! Another test was to leave the urine outside and see if it attracted ants, as ants are attracted to sugar.

Thirst

Because extra water is being lost in the urine, people with uncontrolled diabetes feel very thirsty. Again, this is usually more extreme in type 1. The person might wake up in the night to drink and urinate, or might feel that their mouth is constantly dry. Quenching the thirst with sugary drinks makes the problem even worse.

Thirst
The thirst that is a symptom of diabetes can seem unquenchable.

Tiredness

Tiredness (fatigue) is a common symptom of uncontrolled diabetes, especially when someone is not making enough insulin. The tiredness may be mild or it may be so severe that the person has no energy to do anything any more. Waking in the night to drink or go to the toilet does not help. Tiredness is also a symptom of *low* blood glucose, which can happen when taking insulin or diabetes medications (see page 25). People who have had diabetes for a while can usually tell whether their tiredness is being caused by high or low glucose.

Weight loss

Someone with uncontrolled type 1 diabetes will lose a lot of weight, because they cannot use the glucose they get from food. Instead of being taken in to the cells where it is needed, the glucose passes out in the urine and the calories it contains are lost. Without glucose, the body must break down fat and eventually muscle in order to obtain enough fuel. The effect is the same as going on a starvation diet. If the person does not get insulin they will eventually die.

'I thought, oh good, I'm losing weight. But I felt terrible.'
(Suzanne, 19)

People with type 2 diabetes are able to use glucose to some extent and are often overweight to start with. Weight loss is usually less noticeable, and severe starvation does not occur.

Ketoacidosis

Ketoacidosis is a dangerous condition that is the end result of undiagnosed or uncontrolled type 1 diabetes. The breakdown of fats in the body produces acidic chemical by-products called ketones. Producing small amounts of ketones is normal, especially if you have not eaten for a while or you are dieting to lose weight. Someone with untreated diabetes breaks down so much fat that over time the ketones build up to a dangerous level, causing the blood to become too acidic.

As well as the symptoms of high blood glucose, ketoacidosis causes nausea and vomiting. The breath may smell of pear drops. As the condition becomes more severe, breathing becomes deep and rapid. Eventually the person goes into a coma and will die if not treated.

Diabetes is usually diagnosed and treated before ketoacidosis develops. However, this condition can occur in people with treated diabetes if they stop taking their insulin or if their insulin balance is upset, for example, when they are ill.

Blurred vision

High blood glucose sometimes makes the lens of the eye
swell up, causing blurred vision. This has been described
as like wearing someone else's glasses – everything is out
of focus. Once blood sugar is controlled, vision returns to
normal. Diabetes can also cause long-term damage to the
eyes (see page 43).

Infections

A glucose-rich environment encourages the growth of
infections, especially yeast infection around the urinary
tract, penis and vagina. This is caused by the
microorganism Candida (a type of fungus called a yeast),
and the symptoms are itching, soreness and discharge.
When it affects the vagina it is called thrush. People with
poorly controlled diabetes are also more susceptible to
other infections, especially in the gums, feet and any areas
of damaged skin.

Blurred vision

*Blurred vision is
caused by a change in
shape of the lens of
the eye.*

Jason's summer

Jason,13, was really looking forward to the summer holidays. Six weeks without school! He imagined spending hours playing football in the park with friends, going swimming, and getting to the top level of his favourite computer games. But when the holidays finally came, he just didn't seem to have the energy. For the last week or so he had been really thirsty all the time – but the weather was hot so that was normal, wasn't it? Now he felt really tired, more thirsty than ever (even though it wasn't so hot any more) and was always wanting to pee – even in the night. He was also losing weight. All he felt like doing was lying on the sofa and watching TV. After another week, his mum realized that he wasn't just being lazy and took him to the doctor, who did a blood test. The results came back and she said Jason had diabetes. Jason didn't know what diabetes was, and was scared and confused.

Jason went to the hospital where he had tests. Luckily, he was able to just start his insulin injections, returning daily for checks and dose changes. Had it been left longer, he would have had to stay in hospital for emergency treatment. He was given all the equipment he would need, and the specialist nurse spent a lot of time with him and his mum during those early days, explaining and giving them information about diabetes. They also saw the dietitian, who explained about eating patterns and diabetes.

By the end of the holidays Jason was feeling much better, but inside he was worried about how diabetes would affect his life. At the nurse's suggestion he sent away for a magazine written especially for young people with diabetes. This helped a little.

Testing for diabetes

Diabetes is diagnosed by measuring the glucose level in the blood. The doctor or nurse takes a sample of blood and sends it to a laboratory to be analysed. If the glucose concentration is above a certain level the person is classified as having diabetes (usually after confirmation with a second test). The threshold used depends on whether or not the person has eaten recently. Testing for glucose in the urine is not accurate enough to diagnose diabetes without other tests.

Ron, an undiscovered case of diabetes?

Ron is 50 and works as a bus driver. He admits he is a bit overweight – not really fat, but 'cuddly' as he likes to call it. It's hard to get much exercise when you are driving a bus all day, and at the end of a shift he often feels like some fast food and a few drinks with friends. He has always considered himself a healthy person, and rarely gets sick. Anyway, he hates doctors and hospitals and keeps away from them unless absolutely necessary.

Lately he has been getting tired easily and always seems to be thirsty. When he reaches the end of his route he is desperate to go to the toilet to pee. He puts these things down to his age and then pushes them out of his mind.

Could Ron be one of the millions of people who have diabetes without knowing it?

3 Treating diabetes
Controlling blood glucose

Diabetes cannot yet be cured. Once you have it, you have it for life. The good news is that, with treatment, people with diabetes live normal, active lives. In this chapter we look at the medical aspects of treatment. The other important aspect is diet, which is discussed in Chapter 4.

The treatment needed depends on whether the person has type 1 or type 2 diabetes. People with type 1 need insulin to keep them alive. Beyond this, the goal of treatment is the same for both types: to control the level of glucose in the blood so that it stays as near to normal as possible. It is important to control the blood glucose level in order to:

- stop the symptoms of high blood glucose
- reduce the risk of long-term complications.

Discussing treatment

Doctors can make sure that the treatment given is right for the individual patient, and this will change quite often during the patient's lifetime.

Treating type 1
Insulin

People with type 1 diabetes are unable to make their own insulin, and so they have to take insulin artificially. Insulin is obtained in two ways:

⦿ from the pancreas of pigs or cattle that have been slaughtered for food. This animal insulin is almost the same as human insulin, but not quite.

⦿ from bacteria genetically altered to produce insulin that is chemically identical to the human version. This is called human insulin, and has largely replaced the animal product. The bacteria are grown on a large scale in special production plants, in a process known as fermentation.

Islet of Langerhans

This coloured electron micrograph shows just one cell from the islets of Langerhans, the areas in the pancreas that produce insulin.

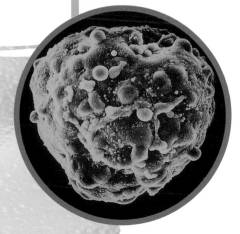

The discovery of insulin

Until the 1920s, type 1 diabetes was a fatal disease. Doctors could do nothing for the children and young people who developed it. They watched helplessly as their patients became progressively thinner and weaker, knowing that within a year they would slip into a coma and die.

In 1901, a pathologist called Eugene Opie discovered that an antidiabetic substance was made in areas of the pancreas known as the islets of Langerhans. A race began to identify and purify this substance. In 1921, a team at Toronto University in Canada succeeded in producing insulin. It was immediately tried out on children who were dying of diabetes in Toronto General Hospital. One was 14-year-old Elizabeth Hughes. She weighed just 52 lbs (24 kilos) and had not long to live. The insulin produced a miraculous recovery, and she lived to be over 70. Frederick Banting and John MacLeod, the scientists who made the first usable insulin, were awarded the Nobel prize in 1923.

Insulin is available in short-acting and longer-acting varieties. Short-acting insulin begins working quickly but its effects last only a few hours. It is usually taken 15-30 minutes before a meal, to deal with the rise in blood glucose that happens after eating. Medium and long-acting insulins work more slowly and last longer. They are often taken once a day to provide background insulin. Many people take a mixture of both types. Patient and doctor work together to decide what insulin routine is best and most convenient for that particular person. Most people take insulin either twice or four times a day.

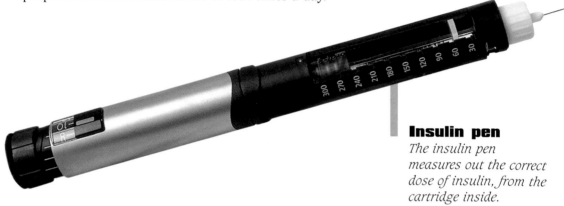

Insulin pen
The insulin pen measures out the correct dose of insulin, from the cartridge inside.

Delivering insulin

Insulin cannot be taken by mouth, as a medicine or tablet, because it would be broken down by the digestive juices in the stomach. Instead it is injected under the skin, where it dissolves into the bloodstream. Injections can be given with a traditional syringe, or using a device that looks like a pen with a fine needle at its tip. People who develop diabetes are taught how to inject themselves, and it soon becomes an everyday part of life.

Insulin can also be given using a pump, a device about the size of a pack of cards that is worn attached to your belt or clothing, like a pager. A continuous small dose is pumped into a fine tube that is attached to a needle left in the skin. Pumps have advantages and disadvantages, but some people prefer them to syringes or pens.

Hannah finds injecting 'second nature'

Hannah was diagnosed with type 1 diabetes when she was 11. 'When the doctor said I would have to inject myself twice a day for the rest of my life, I just burst into tears,' she remembers. 'The first few times I tried it I was terrified, and it was painful because I wasn't very good at it. On top of that, I had to prick my finger every day to test my blood. I hated it.' That was four years ago. 'Now it's just second nature to me,' Hannah says. 'I reckon I'm better at giving injections than most doctors! Friends say "Yuck, how can you do that?" They think I'm really brave, but I just get on with it. The needles are really fine, and once you know what you're doing it doesn't usually hurt at all. But I wish there was a way of monitoring your blood where you didn't have to prick your finger.'

Hannah has an insulin pen. 'It's more convenient when you're out because you don't have to carry a separate bottle and syringe. And you can inject yourself quickly and easily without anyone noticing.'

Treating type 2 diabetes

The treatment needed for type 2 diabetes varies from person to person. Some people find they can control their blood glucose just by switching to a healthier diet, taking more exercise and losing weight. This often works in the early stages, but type 2 is a progressive condition that tends to get worse over the years. Sooner or later, most of those affected will need to take medication.

There are various drugs available to help control blood glucose. Some stimulate the pancreas to produce more insulin, while others help the body to use insulin more effectively. Some are taken with meals, others just once or twice a day. Sometimes more than one type is needed. The drugs are used together with a healthy diet, not as a replacement.

About 30 per cent of people with type 2 diabetes need to move on to insulin at some time, often after using tablets for many years. Insulin treatment is discussed under type 1 diabetes (pages 21-23).

Monitoring blood glucose

Everyone with diabetes – whether type 1 or type 2 – needs to monitor their blood glucose regularly to make sure that their treatment is working well. The more tightly glucose levels are controlled, the lower the risk of developing complications like heart trouble, eye problems or kidney damage.

Blood glucose is tested by pricking the finger with a small blade or stapler and putting a drop of blood on a testing strip. The strip then changes colour, the shade depending on how much glucose is present. The result is interpreted by comparing the strip with a colour chart. Also available are small electric meters which interpret the strip automatically and display a glucose reading. The very latest devices can test blood glucose without breaking the skin, though the readings

'Testing can be really annoying, and sometimes I just can't be bothered. But I know it's worth it in the long run. I mean, it's your future health you're talking about.' (Lee, college student)

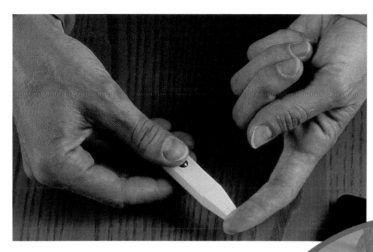

A finger-prick device is used to produce a drop of blood. The blood is put onto a test strip, which changes colour according to how much glucose is in the blood. Matching the strip against a colour scale shows whether the glucose level is low, average or high.

may not be as accurate as with traditional finger-prick methods. If glucose is higher or lower than normal, then treatment or eating can be adjusted. Keeping a diary of the results gives a longer-term picture of how well blood glucose is being controlled.

Hypos

Controlling blood glucose is a balancing act, normally orchestrated by the finely tuned release of natural insulin. People who use insulin injections or anti-diabetes tablets don't have this fine-tuning, and sometimes their glucose level dips too low. This is called hypoglycaemia, and a person who is hypoglycaemic is described as having a 'hypo'. It is also sometimes called an insulin reaction.

The most common cause of hypos is missing or delaying a meal. It is therefore important for people with diabetes to eat regularly, with snacks between meals if necessary. Hypos can also be caused by too much insulin, drinking too much alcohol, or by taking strenuous exercise without eating beforehand. Nobody can balance their glucose control perfectly all the time, so occasional hypos are usually an unavoidable part of life with diabetes.

Symptoms

The symptoms of hypoglycaemia include shaking, dizziness, sweating, heart palpitations, anxiety, going pale, tingling lips and blurred vision. It becomes difficult to concentrate, and the person may get irritable and moody. These are warning signs. People with diabetes (and their close friends and families) learn to recognize when a hypo is coming on, and can usually take action before it becomes worse. If the blood glucose drops lower, the person may start acting strangely, or may laugh or cry for no apparent reason. In severe hypoglycaemia people become confused and can no longer think for themselves, and will eventually become unconscious.

Understanding Dad

Stephen's dad has had diabetes since before Stephen was born. 'Usually he's really laid back,' says Stephen, 'except when he has a hypo. Sometimes it's when he's had a beer or at weekends when we have lunch late. He starts getting niggly, telling us off for nothing or going on about what a mess the house is, when usually he doesn't care. My sister and I think "uh-oh, Dad's getting hypo …". My Mum says "Have some chocolate, John", and he'll get really annoyed and tell her to stop fussing and leave him alone. But she knows he needs it. She usually pours a glass of Coke and just leaves it out, and he drinks it when he thinks she isn't looking. After that he eats a sandwich or something, and then he's fine. Dad having diabetes is no big deal. He's never been any different from any of my friends' dads – except he's fitter than most of them because he takes better care of himself.'

Hypos are rarely fatal, because after a while the body's own compensation systems will release more glucose into the blood and bring the person back to consciousness. However, a hypo could be very dangerous, for example if it happened when driving a car or operating machinery. A hypo can also be embarrassing and inconvenient if it happens at an awkward time – say in a meeting or during a night out. Hypos can be quite frightening and upsetting, but for most people they are usually mild and no more than a nuisance.

What to do

Someone having a hypo needs to eat something sugary to get glucose into their blood quickly. This could be glucose tablets, sweets or chocolate, jam or a sugary drink. People with diabetes are advised to keep a source of sugar handy wherever they go. Friends and family should be aware of the signs and suggest a sugary snack if the person is not thinking clearly enough to realize they need it. If someone passes out from a hypo, call an ambulance. Do not attempt to give them food or drink, as this could cause choking. Severe hypos are treated with injections of the hormone glucagon, which releases glucose from the liver. Some people carry a glucagon injecting kit with them.

Act quickly

If someone passes out from a hypo, call quickly for help.

Check-ups and support

People with diabetes have a regular check-up every 6-12 months to see how well their treatment is working and to check for early signs of complications. The check-up is also a chance to discuss any questions or problems that have arisen. Diabetes is treated by teams of healthcare professionals, including specialist doctors (diabetologists), family doctors, specialist nurses, dietitians, chiropodists and eye specialists. Special clinics are run for children and teenagers.

Diabetes check-up

A specialist nurse shows a young patient with diabetes how to look after his feet.

Preventing diabetes

As always, prevention is better than cure. Recent studies have shown that those at high risk of developing type 2 diabetes can dramatically reduce their chances of getting the disease if they eat less fat, lose around 15 lbs (7 kilos) and take exercise equivalent to walking for 30 minutes a day. Other trials are focusing on people with genes thought to put them at risk of type 1 diabetes, to see if treatments such as particular vitamins or low doses of insulin can prevent the disease from developing.

Future developments

Scientists around the world are working to develop new treatments for diabetes. Many believe that a cure will be found in the foreseeable future. Research is following various different routes, for example:

- transplanting insulin-producing islet cells from donated pancreases into people who can no longer make their own insulin. A small number of people have been given transplants so far, with promising results. But there are drawbacks, including the long-term side effects of anti-rejection drugs, which must be taken for life after any transplant.

- using genetic engineering techniques to try to make cells that produce insulin.

- finding the genes that make people susceptible to diabetes. This should open the way for new treatments, and might make it possible to prevent diabetes developing. Several such genes have already been discovered.

- carrying out trials of inhalers that deliver insulin to the lungs. From the lungs it is absorbed into the bloodstream. This would provide a welcome alternative to injections and pens. Skin patches and tablets are also being developed, but there are serious obstacles to be overcome.

Identifying genes
These test tubes of DNA in a laboratory refrigerator are part of a human gene bank. They are a valuable resource for scientists looking for the genes that put people at risk of diabetes.

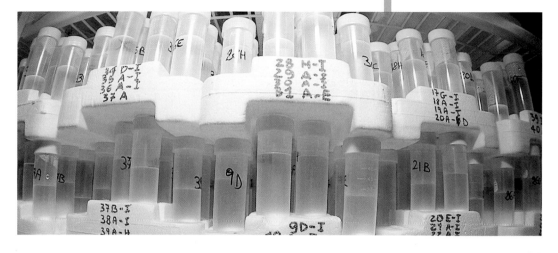

4 Diabetes and diet
A healthy balance

Up until the 1980s, people with diabetes were told to follow a special diet. In an effort to control blood glucose, sugar and foods containing it were banned and the amount of starchy food eaten was restricted. All that has now changed. Scientific studies showed that restricting carbohydrate was not beneficial to diabetes control. Instead, people with diabetes follow the same healthy eating guidelines that apply to everyone else.

What is food made of?

Food contains three basic types of nutrient: carbohydrates, fats and proteins. It also contains vitamins and minerals.

Carbohydrates fall into two classes: simple and complex. Simple carbohydrates are called sugars, and their main function is to provide energy. They include sucrose (the sugar we buy in shops) and fructose

Enjoy yourself
People with diabetes don't need to worry about a special diet. A healthy, balanced diet is best for everyone.

'I don't have to be "good" about food all the time. If we're out and I fancy an ice cream my friends go "Oh, are you sure you should be having that?" and that really annoys me.'
(Kirsty, 14)

Fibre and whole grains

Although it is not absorbed by the body, dietary fibre has many beneficial effects.

- *It helps prevent constipation and related digestive problems.*
- *It's filling, so you are less likely to over-eat .*
- *One type, called **soluble fibre**, slows down the absorption of glucose (helpful for people with diabetes) and can lower the level of cholesterol in the blood. High blood cholesterol increases the risk of heart attack.*

***Insoluble fibre** comes from the cell walls and outer skin of plants and grains, and is found in fruit, vegetables and wholegrain cereals. The outer layer of cereal grains is removed when they are milled to their white form, taking with it the fibre and many of the vitamins and minerals. Examples of wholegrain foods are wholemeal bread, wholewheat breakfast cereals, brown rice and wholemeal pasta. The best sources of **soluble** fibre are fruits, beans, oats and barley. Edible gums like guar gum, which are used as thickeners in many foods, are forms of soluble fibre.*

(the natural sugar found in fruit). Complex carbohydrates are found in plant foods and can be either digestible (starch) or indigestible (dietary fibre). Starch is an energy source and fibre provides bulk to help food move through the intestines easily. Sugars and starch are broken down into glucose – the simplest form of sugar – during digestion. Starch takes longer to break down, and so it does not push blood glucose up as rapidly.

Fats are found in animal foods (meat, eggs and dairy products) and in plants, where they are called oils. They are classified as either saturated (most animal fats) or unsaturated (most plant oils). Too much saturated fat is linked to heart disease. Fats and oils have two main functions: they are a concentrated source of energy, and they contain fatty acids, which our bodies need for making cell membranes, hormones and the chemicals of the immune system.

Starch

Pasta, bread, potatoes and bananas are some useful starchy foods.

Proteins are made up of chemicals called amino acids. They are present in most foods. Animal products are the richest source, but there are also good amounts of proteins in beans, peas, lentils, grains and nuts. Proteins form the basic structure of our skin, muscle, connective tissue and organs, and have many other vital functions in the body.

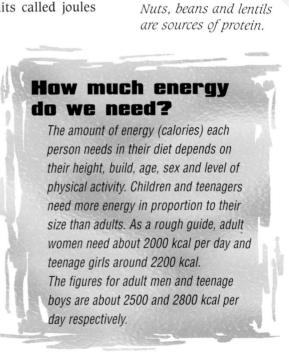

Full of beans!
Nuts, beans and lentils are sources of protein.

Energy and body weight

We need energy to drive all the physical and chemical processes of our bodies, and to move our muscles and do work. Energy is measured in imperial units called calories and kilocalories or in metric units called joules and kilojoules.

All our energy comes from food. The richest source is fat or oil, at 9 kilocalories (kcal) per gram. Carbohydrates and protein contain 4 kcal per gram and alcohol 7 kcal per gram. Not all the energy in food is used straight away. Some of it is stored by the body in the chemical bonds of fat molecules, ready to be released again when needed. If we take in more energy than we use up, our fat stores increase and we put on weight. If we take in less energy than we use, the fat is broken down and we become thinner and lighter.

How much energy do we need?

The amount of energy (calories) each person needs in their diet depends on their height, build, age, sex and level of physical activity. Children and teenagers need more energy in proportion to their size than adults. As a rough guide, adult women need about 2000 kcal per day and teenage girls around 2200 kcal.

The figures for adult men and teenage boys are about 2500 and 2800 kcal per day respectively.

Weight-watching

Eighty per cent of people who develop type 2 diabetes are overweight. Being overweight is unhealthy for anyone, but is especially bad for those with diabetes. For this group, losing weight helps to control blood glucose by enabling the body to use insulin more effectively. It also helps prevent high blood pressure and lowers the risk of heart attacks and strokes.

To lose weight, you must eat fewer calories than your body uses up. The best way to cut down on calories is to eat less fat, because fat contains more calories than any other food group. Foods containing a lot of added sugar should also be avoided. A diet that is low in fat and sugar and high in starchy food is a good way of keeping to a healthy weight. People with more weight to lose may need advice from their doctor or a dietitian, so that their diabetes treatment can be adjusted to fit in with their slimming diet.

Taking regular exercise is just as important as diet, as it burns up extra calories that would otherwise be stored as fat.

Keep fit!
Exercise burns up food energy and stops it being stored as fat.

Diet matters

For everyone, a healthy diet lowers the risk of cancer, and helps you look better and feel fitter. If you have diabetes healthy eating is even more important. The right food choices and eating habits help to:

- prevent blood glucose going too high or too low
- control weight, which in turn helps diabetes control
- reduce the risk of long-term complications from diabetes
- keep the heart healthy (diabetes increases the risk of heart disease).

People with diabetes do need to think more carefully than most about what they eat and when. The aim is to balance the amount of insulin or tablets used with the amount of food eaten. The easiest way to do this is to have a regular eating pattern, and to include roughly the same amount of carbohydrate in each meal. Missing a meal can let the blood glucose drop too low, causing symptoms like dizziness, loss of concentration and even collapse: this is known as a 'hypo' (see page 25). On the other hand, eating something sugary like a bar of chocolate could send the blood glucose too high unless medication is adjusted carefully. Over time, high blood glucose causes serious complications (see Chapter 5).

"I always carry a snack with me. Sometimes I have to eat in class, but I'm allowed because I've got diabetes. If I'm out, taking a snack means I don't have to worry about always being home early to eat."
(Darren, 12)

Some people who take insulin are advised to eat carbohydrate-rich snacks between meals to keep their blood glucose up and prevent hypos.

Snack attack!
Examples of carbohydrate-rich snacks include fresh or dried fruit, a couple of biscuits, a cereal bar, a sandwich or a scone.

What is a healthy diet?
A healthy diet contains a wide, balanced variety of foods and is:

- rich in starchy foods and fibre
- low in fat, sugar and salt
- high in fruit and vegetables.

People with diabetes have sessions with a dietitian to work out an eating pattern that not only helps their glucose control but also suits their individual lifestyle, likes and dislikes.

Sugary and fatty foods should be kept to a minimum. Too many can cause health problems and weight gain. They include sweets, chocolate, biscuits, fizzy drinks, butter and margarine, fried foods, burgers, crisps and pastry.

Protein foods: two portions a day will give all the protein you need. Foods in this group are meat, fish, eggs, dairy foods, beans, lentils, nuts and soya products like veggieburgers.

Milk and dairy foods are sources of calcium and some vitamins, and we need at least one portion a day. Choosing semi-skimmed milk and low-fat yoghurt is a good way of keeping the fat content down.

Starchy foods – bread, cereals, potatoes, rice, pasta – should form the main part of each meal, along with vegetables. Eat plenty of whole-grain foods, e.g. wholemeal bread, wholegrain breakfast cereals.

Fruit and vegetables: at least five portions each day. Fruit juice and tinned or frozen items can all count towards the five. A portion is a good-sized helping, not just a couple of lettuce leaves!

Artificial sweeteners and 'diabetic' foods

Thanks to artificial sweeteners, foods can be made to taste sweet without the use of sugars. These sweeteners are made from chemicals with an extremely powerful sweet taste, so that only a tiny amount is needed. They contain no calories. The main artificial sweeteners are aspartame, saccharin and acesulfame K, and they are found mostly in 'diet' drinks and in low-calorie yoghurts and desserts. These products can be useful in diabetes as they provide variety in the diet without affecting blood glucose.

So-called diabetic foods were common in the shops until a few years ago, and some are still sold. They are sweet foods like chocolates, biscuits, cakes and jams that are made with alternatives to ordinary sugar (sucrose). The usual sweeteners are sorbitol or fructose, both of which contain calories and behave like sugars in the body. These foods are not recommended because they are expensive and offer no benefit to people with diabetes.

Healthy options: cooking and diabetes

Diabetes doesn't mean giving up on your favourite recipes – even the sweet ones! Many dishes can be made successfully with much less sugar and fat than stated in the recipe. For example, cakes can be made with half the sugar, although they will not keep as long as usual. In fruit cakes, dried fruit can replace sugar completely. Artificial sweeteners cannot be used in cooked dishes because they don't provide the bulk required to make the recipe work. They also break down at high temperatures to give a bitter taste.

Not so sweet
A delicious fruit cake can be made without any added sugar.

Small changes can make all the difference when it comes to cutting down on fat. Here are some ideas:

- Use skimmed or semi-skimmed milk.
- Try out lower-fat cheeses such as edam or reduced-fat cheddar, or use small amounts of strongly flavoured cheese.
- Use low-fat spreads instead of butter or margarine, and spread them thinly.
- Choose lean cuts of meat, or trim off the fat.
- Poach, bake or grill instead of frying.
- Fill up on vegetables and fruit if you are hungry.
- Snack on fruit instead of crisps or biscuits.

Recipe Idea 1

Salmon fishcakes and low-fat tartar sauce (serves 3)

For the fishcakes:
350g mashed potato
50g sweetcorn
150g cooked or tinned salmon
2 tablespoons fresh coriander, chopped
1 red chilli, deseeded and chopped
salt and freshly ground black pepper

For the sauce:
2 tablespoons virtually fat-free mayonnaise
1 tablespoon light crème fraiche
2 tablespoons fresh parsley, chopped
2 tablespoons capers, drained and roughly chopped
1 teaspoon horseradish sauce

Combine all the fishcake ingredients in a large bowl. With flour on your hands, form the mixture into six cakes, then chill for 15 minutes. Brush with a little oil and grill for 3-4 minutes on each side, until golden.
For the sauce, mix all the ingredients together well.
Serve with some starchy food such as a baked potato, and plenty of vegetables or salad.
(Note: oily fish such as salmon, mackerel, sardines and tuna contain omega-3 fatty acids, which can protect against heart disease. Eating at least one portion a week is recommended.)

Recipe Idea 2

Apple and oat slices (makes 16)

450g cooking apples, peeled, cored and
    sliced
2 tablespoons caster sugar
250g reduced fat mono-unsaturated spread
    (eg one based on olive oil)
2 tablespoons honey
175g plain wholemeal flour
1 teaspoon baking powder
200g rolled oats
50g chopped hazelnuts

Pre-heat the oven to 180°C. Put the apples in a saucepan with the sugar and two tablespoons of water. Bring to the boil and simmer gently until a pulp is formed. Remove from the heat. Melt the spread in a large saucepan and stir in the honey. Remove from the heat and stir in the flour, baking powder, oats and nuts. Press half the oat mixture into the base of a shallow 18 x 27 cm baking tin. Spoon the apple mixture over. Crumble the remaining oat mixture over the fruit and press down gently. Bake for 30 minutes or until evenly browned. After cooling slightly in the tin, cut into 16 bars and cool on a wire rack. Store in the fridge. (Note: these are a delicious alternative to commercial cereal bars, many of which are high in fat and sugar.)

Recipes from Diabetes UK, used with permission.

Alcohol

Adults with diabetes can drink moderate amounts of alcohol if they want to. Alcohol is measured in units – 1 unit equals half a pint of beer or lager, one pub measure of spirits or a standard glass of wine. The maximum recommended amounts are 14 units a week for adult women and 21 for adult men – whether they have diabetes or not. Of course, it's not a good idea to drink a week's worth in one go! Diabetes means taking extra care when drinking because alcohol increases the risk of having a hypo (see page 25). The advice is to have plenty of starchy snacks before, during and after drinking.

1 unit of alcohol is equivalent to:

half a pint (285 ml) of ordinary strength beer, lager or cider

1 measure (25ml) of spirits

1 standard glass (125ml) of ordinary wine

The dietitian

Ellen is a State Registered Dietitian. She is trained in both the scientific and practical aspects of diet and nutrition. Based at a large hospital, she gives advice on diet to patients with a range of illnesses such as kidney disease, heart disease and food intolerances, and to people who are seriously overweight. For two days a week she is attached to the diabetes clinic. 'Seeing people with diabetes is a big part of my work,' she says. 'At diabetes clinics you get all shapes and sizes and all age groups, from very young children and their parents through to elderly people. Some of them have just been diagnosed, and they are often anxious and confused. First I go through their current eating patterns and their lifestyle. Then I advise on any changes that are needed and help them come up with a food plan that suits them. After that I see them at their regular clinic visits and we discuss how they are doing and any questions they might have. People with diabetes often need to lose weight, and I help them with that as well.'

The budding chef

Sean is a keen cook and wants to train as a chef when he leaves school. He often cooks the meal at home: 'It gets me out of the washing-up!' he says. When Sean developed diabetes, he and his mum decided to make the whole family's diet more healthy. 'We have more rice, pasta and potatoes than we used to,' he explains, 'and more vegetables and fruit. We still have things like sausage and chips sometimes, but Mum buys the low-fat ones.'
His favourite dishes include

- ⚫ *spicy chicken and vegetable curry with rice – 'take-away curries are really fatty, so we make our own most of the time'*
- ⚫ *baked potatoes with mince and bean chilli*
- ⚫ *tuna, red-pepper and tomato pasta with parmesan – 'parmesan gives a strong cheese flavour without too much fat'*
- ⚫ *fruit salad – 'just mix up all your favourite fruits'*
- ⚫ *good old baked beans and poached eggs on wholemeal toast.*

5 Health risks from diabetes

Long-term complications

Better control
Treatment has improved and people live longer and can stay fitter than in the past. So complications leading to the amputation of a foot or leg are less common and more avoidable.

High blood glucose is not just a meaningless test result. It poses a serious risk to health, both in the short term and over a period of years. We have already discussed the short-term effects – thirst, excessive urination, weight loss, tiredness and blurred vision (see Chapter 2). In this chapter we will look at the long-term damage caused by a high level of glucose in the blood.

Diabetes is a major cause of disability and premature death in those who have had it for several years or more. It can affect the eyes, kidneys, nervous system, heart and blood vessels. These problems are especially common in older people who spent many years with diabetes when the condition could not be controlled as well as it can be today. The good news is that careful glucose control can dramatically reduce the risk of developing complications. If caught early, most complications can now be treated before they become severe.

Good control gets results – official!

Keeping blood glucose as close to normal as possible really does pay off. Proof of this came from a 10-year study ending in 1993. 1441 people with type 1 diabetes were split into two groups, half following an intensive treatment routine and the rest sticking to ordinary insulin treatment. In the intensive group, the aim was to keep blood glucose at almost normal (non-diabetic) levels. This was achieved by using more frequent insulin injections and adjusting treatment or diet following self-testing of glucose levels four times a day.

Doctors then compared the rate at which diabetic complications developed or progressed in each group. The results were dramatic, with the intensive group showing a 60 per cent reduction compared with the others. However, there were drawbacks. Hypos were more frequent in the intensive group, and often occurred without warning. In addition, intensive control requires a lot of commitment and will not suit everyone. People with diabetes need to consider all the issues with their care team and work out a level of control that they are comfortable with.

Cardiovascular disease

Cardiovascular disease involves a build-up of hard, fatty deposits in the arteries that supply blood to the heart and brain. It is also known as atherosclerosis or hardening of the arteries. Over the years, the deposits narrow the space inside the artery and make it more difficult for blood to get through. Sometimes a blood clot develops and blocks it completely. If this occurs in the arteries supplying the heart muscle (the coronary arteries), the heart is starved of oxygen and part of the muscle dies. This is a heart attack. If a large enough area of the heart is affected, the person will die.

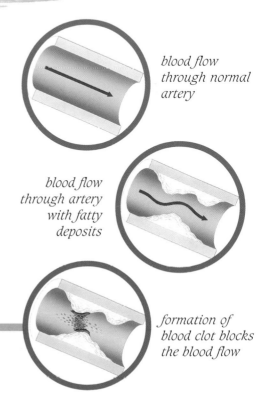

blood flow through normal artery

blood flow through artery with fatty deposits

formation of blood clot blocks the blood flow

Narrowing of the arteries
This process can lead to a heart attack or to a stroke.

Blockage of an artery in the brain is called a stroke. Part of the brain dies from lack of oxygen. The area affected can be so small that the stroke goes unnoticed, or large enough to kill. People who survive strokes are often left with a disability such as weakness down one side or speech difficulties.

Cardiovascular disease is a leading cause of death and disability in the Western world, and the risk for people with diabetes is four times greater than for the population as a whole. For everyone, the main risk factors for cardiovascular disease are:

- high blood pressure
- high blood cholesterol
- smoking
- obesity
- lack of exercise.

The more of these factors you have, the greater your risk. Having diabetes, particularly type 2, is linked to all of them (except smoking), but is also thought to be a risk factor in itself. People with diabetes – and everyone else – can reduce their risk of cardiovascular disease by:

- stopping smoking – probably the most important step you can take
- eating a low-fat, fibre-rich diet; this has been proven to lower cholesterol and help control weight
- losing weight if necessary
- taking regular exercise
- having regular check-ups to monitor blood pressure and cholesterol levels, and taking medication to control them if required.

Stroke

A stroke left this woman with a speech disorder called aphasia. It affects the ability to put thoughts into words. At a speech therapy session, she tries to name the objects in some pictures.

Jim starts a new regime

Jim has recently been diagnosed with type 2 diabetes at the age of 48. His doctor is particularly concerned because Jim is overweight and has high blood pressure and high cholesterol, all of which increase the risk of heart disease. What's more, Jim's father died of a heart attack in his fifties. 'The doctor told me that if I didn't do something, I had a good chance of going the same way as my father,' he says. 'That was pretty scary.' Encouraged by his wife, Jim decided to take action. He began walking to and from the railway station each day instead of taking the bus. At lunchtime in the canteen, he replaced his usual choice of pizza or fish and chips with baked potatoes, salads, chicken, grilled meat or poached fish. Instead of a mid-morning doughnut, he has a banana or a couple of crackers. 'It's hard work,' he admits, 'but I've already lost some weight and I'm starting to feel fitter. I've got more energy.' His cholesterol is down too, and the doctor has put him on a lower dose of diabetes control tablets. 'Diabetes has been a wake-up call for me,' says Jim. 'From now on I'm going to look after my body instead of taking it for granted.'

Eye damage

Diabetes is the most common cause of blindness in adults in the developed world. High levels of glucose damage the tiny blood vessels that supply the retina – the area inside the eye that is responsible for vision. They become blocked and start to bleed or leak – a process known as retinopathy. It can be detected by looking into the eye with an instrument called an ophthalmoscope. The doctor first uses eye drops to dilate the pupil so that he or she can see in properly.

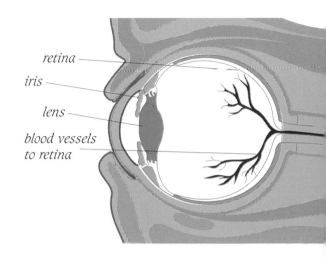

retina

iris

lens

blood vessels to retina

Eye examination

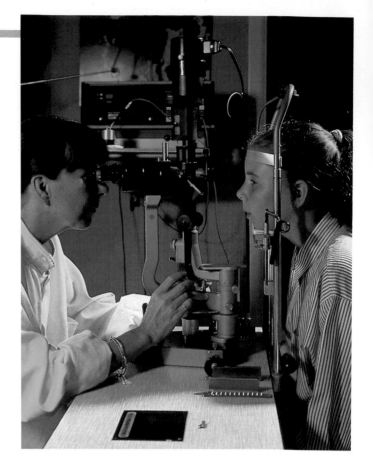

An optician looks into the eyepiece of a slit-lamp ophthalmoscope, to examine the inside of a patient's eye. The ophthalmoscope sends a beam of light into the eye and contains magnifying lenses so the optician can see where the beam falls.

Most people who have had diabetes for 5-10 years or more show some sign of retinopathy. This is usually a type called background retinopathy, which does not affect vision and is no cause for alarm. However, in a few people the condition progresses. As more vessels get blocked, the blood supply to the retina decreases and new vessels are grown to try to compensate. The new blood vessels are fragile and break easily, causing bleeding into the eye and the formation of tiny scars. A large bleed causes loss of vision in the affected eye. Although the vision may clear over the next few weeks as the blood drains out, bleeding may happen again. A build-up of damage can lead to permanent loss of sight, either partial or complete.

Treatment

Fortunately, progressive retinopathy can be successfully treated if caught early. A specialist doctor uses a finely focused laser beam to seal off the new blood vessels before they bleed into the eye. This is usually painless and prevents severe loss of sight in about 90 per cent of cases. That is why everyone who has had diabetes for 5-10 years or more should have an eye examination each year. (This is not the same as an eye test, which picks up long- or short-sightedness.) Now that this treatment is available, diabetic blindness will become much less common.

The nervous system

The nervous system coordinates everything our bodies do. Nerve cells originate in the brain and spinal cord, from where they spread out in bundles to the internal organs and to every part of the body, branching as they go to form an ever-finer network. Some control the movement of muscles, some carry signals that provide our senses of touch and pain, and others perform automatic functions like telling the lungs to breathe or moving the intestines so that food passes through.

High blood glucose over a long period can damage nerve cells, a process called neuropathy. The most common problem is damage to the tiny nerves at the outer extremities of the body. This is called peripheral neuropathy, and usually affects the feet. It normally begins with numbness or tingling in the toes, and over a period of years spreads up the feet and into the ankles and lower legs. Many people who have had years of poorly controlled diabetes will suffer from neuropathy to some extent. As well as numbness and tingling, it can cause recurrent, sometimes severe pain. The area may become over-sensitive, so that even the touch of bedclothes is unpleasant.

Less commonly, neuropathy affects other nerves as well. For example, there may be problems with the nerves that control erections in men and sexual arousal in women. The digestive system can also be affected.

Nerve fibre
Nerve fibres reach almost every part of the body. Here a nerve makes contact with the muscle cells it controls.

Treatment

Neuropathy cannot be cured. The painful stage is temporary – though it may last 6-18 months. Doctors can prescribe various different drugs to relieve the pain. Better glucose control will slow down the progression of neuropathy.

Foot problems

It may seem strange to connect diabetes with the feet, but foot ulcers are the most common reason for people with diabetes to be admitted to hospital. An ulcer is a wound or sore that goes deep into the skin and is slow to heal. Diabetes can affect both the nerves and the blood supply of the feet – this is more likely to happen if someone has had diabetes for many years and if glucose control is poor.

'One night I took off my sock and it was covered in blood. I had walked round all day with a drawing pin stuck in my foot, and I didn't feel anything.'
(Jean, shop assistant)

Neuropathy dulls the sense of feeling in the feet, so they can be injured without the person noticing. For example, a new pair of shoes might rub the foot raw without any pain

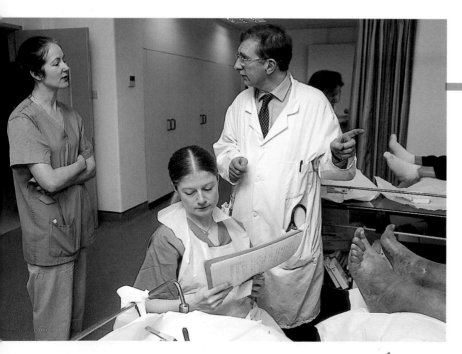

Foot clinic
Staff at a foot clinic for people with diabetes are skilled at treating the complications that result from neuropathy and poor circulation.

being felt, or an object could get stuck in the foot and be left there. Any foot wound or infection is particularly serious if diabetes has damaged the small blood vessels that supply the area. A poor blood supply (also called poor circulation) makes it harder for injured tissue to heal and reduces the immune system's ability to fight off infection. The result can be a sore that goes septic and won't heal. In the worst cases, the affected toe, foot or leg may have to be amputated (removed). This normally only happens in older people whose circulation is poor.

Treatment

People with diabetes must take any foot wound or infection seriously and see their doctor straight away if there are any signs of redness, swelling, heat or pain. Infections are treated with antibiotics, which may have to be given in hospital through an intravenous drip.

Diabetic ulcer

Ulcers on the feet are associated with diabetes, but special care can be taken to avoid them.

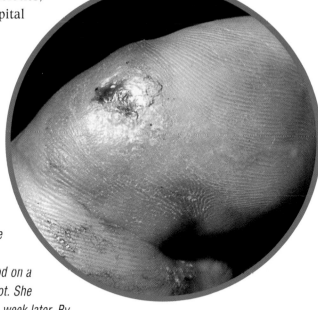

A diabetic foot ulcer

Alice is 74 and was diagnosed with type 2 diabetes 15 years ago. Because she was already showing signs of nerve damage, her doctor said she had probably had diabetes for about ten years before that. Over the years, Alice lost more and more of the feeling in her teet. Then one day she trod on a large splinter, which got stuck in her foot. She didn't notice until it began to swell up a week later. By then the infection had taken hold, and an open sore developed. Three months later, and despite a stay in hospital, it is still not fully healed. The doctor blames poor circulation, saying that not enough blood is reaching the wound. This is common in older people but has probably been made worse by diabetes. The chiropodist visits regularly to change the dressing, but Alice can't walk on the foot and finds it difficult to manage at home, even with the help of her daughter who comes in when she can. Her foot is getting better, but it's a slow process.

The person may be advised to rest the foot completely while it heals. A slow-healing wound or ulcer will need regular dressing by a nurse or chiropodist (someone trained in looking after the feet, also called a podiatrist). Dead tissue may have to be removed, sometimes under anaesthetic.

With foot problems, prevention is definitely better than cure. Checking the feet for early signs of nerve damage is part of the regular check-up at the diabetes clinic.

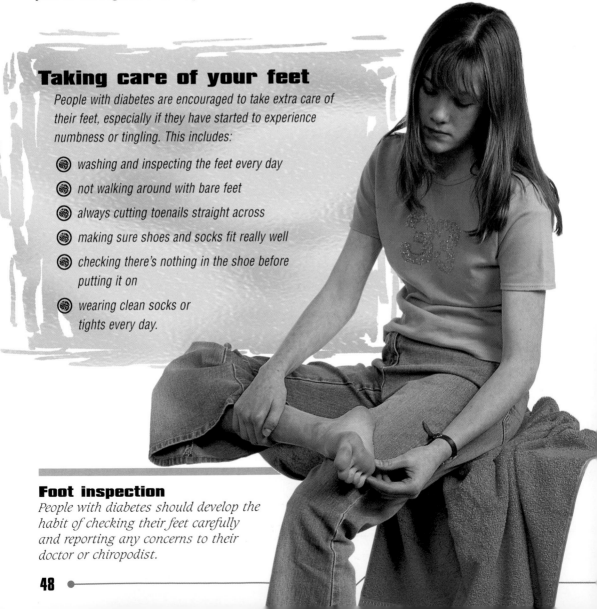

Taking care of your feet

People with diabetes are encouraged to take extra care of their feet, especially if they have started to experience numbness or tingling. This includes:

- *washing and inspecting the feet every day*
- *not walking around with bare feet*
- *always cutting toenails straight across*
- *making sure shoes and socks fit really well*
- *checking there's nothing in the shoe before putting it on*
- *wearing clean socks or tights every day.*

Foot inspection

People with diabetes should develop the habit of checking their feet carefully and reporting any concerns to their doctor or chiropodist.

Kidney damage

High blood glucose over a long period can also damage the small blood vessels in the kidney. This is called nephropathy, and eventually affects about 25 per cent of people with diabetes to some extent. Like the other complications of diabetes, it is becoming less common as glucose control improves.

The kidney acts as a filter to clean the blood of harmful waste products. This is done in millions of little units called nephrons, which consist of a blood vessel surrounded by a long tube in which urine is formed. In nephropathy the walls of the blood vessels get thicker and no longer work properly. Eventually they get blocked. If this happens to enough nephrons, waste products begin to build up in the body.

Nephropathy produces no symptoms until it is far advanced. The first sign is protein in the urine, which can show up many years before the kidney fails. Water starts to build up in the body, causing swollen ankles (ankle swelling is a symptom of various other conditions as well). In severe cases the kidney fails completely. The person then needs either a kidney transplant or renal dialysis to keep them alive. Renal dialysis is an artificial way of filtering the blood, using either a kidney machine or a bag of fluid that is carried inside the abdomen and regularly drained.

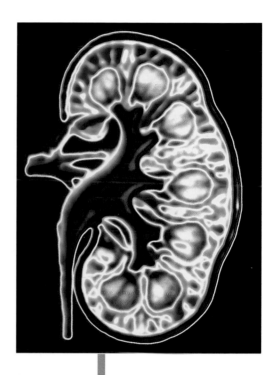

A healthy kidney
We have two kidneys. Blood enters through the renal artery (left) and passes into the outer cortex, shown in blue. There, excess water and wastes turn into urine, which drains through the medulla (shown in yellow-orange) into a tube (red) leading to the bladder.

Treatment

People with diabetes have their urine tested for protein at least once a year. If kidney damage is found early, its progress can usually be slowed down or stopped. Taking extra care to control blood glucose is important, and the person may be advised to cut down the amount of protein and salt that they eat. Drugs are prescribed to control high blood pressure, because it puts added strain on the kidney.

6 Living with diabetes
Planning and support

Diabetes is a serious condition, but once treated it does not stop people leading normal, active lives. With a little planning and the right information and support, they can be in control of their diabetes – rather than letting it control them. It takes some thought and organization, but most people become good at juggling their food, medication and blood testing so that they can take everyday life in their stride.

Preparation
Many people use a small electric meter to get a glucose reading of their blood. Then they can adapt their insulin dose or diet, especially before extra exercise.

Looking after yourself

Everyone needs to look after themselves to stay healthy, but people with diabetes are encouraged to take a little extra care. Good diabetes care means:

- making your diet healthy
- testing yourself regularly and adjusting medication or diet accordingly
- keeping to a healthy weight
- exercising regularly
- not smoking
- having regular check-ups at the diabetes clinic.

All these points are discussed in more detail elsewhere in the book.

'When I went back to school after I got diabetes, I was worried what to tell people. It was embarrassing. I thought people would think I was weird, but everyone was fine about it except for a couple of people, and they're just idiots anyway.'
(Alex, 15)

Diabetes and school

There is probably at least one student or teacher at your school who has diabetes. It's important that schools and teachers understand about diabetes, so it's a good idea for affected students and their parents to discuss it with the appropriate person. They can then explain about blood testing and injections, why the student might sometimes need to eat in class, and what to do if he or she has a hypo.

Students with diabetes can take part in school trips and after-school activities, but it will probably mean thinking ahead about how to adjust their meals, snacks and insulin. This means that they are often better-organized than the average child or teenager!

Diabetes and work

People with diabetes work in all walks of life, including physically strenuous jobs and those with irregular hours. However, there are a few jobs that people who take insulin are not allowed to do. These vary from country to country, but include things like airline pilot, some driving jobs and being in the armed forces.

Many employers have no experience of diabetes, and some may be wary about offering a job to an affected person. Diabetes organizations can offer advice on how and when to tell employers about the condition; keeping it secret is not a good idea. People with well-controlled diabetes often have qualities that employers are looking for: coping with diabetes makes them well-organized and self-reliant, and because they take good care of themselves they may actually take less time off sick than someone without diabetes!

Interview
People with diabetes must decide how and when to tell a potential employer about it.

The high-flier

Simon is a lawyer with a top firm. It's a stressful lifestyle, with long hours and tight deadlines, but he enjoys the 'buzz' of office life, not to mention the big salary that goes with it. He has always pushed himself hard, getting high grades at school and a degree from a leading university. He also loves hockey and plays for a team. 'I've had diabetes since I was eight,' he says, 'and I've never let it stop me doing what I want. Maybe it made me even more determined to prove myself.'

Simon's working days are unpredictable. 'One day I might be travelling to see a client, the next I might be in court all day. There are also a lot of business lunches. It's not the ideal environment for good diabetes control, but there is a way round everything if you look for it. My diabetes care team have been really good in helping me find the best type of insulin to cope with my lifestyle and advising me on eating and testing. It is an added stress, but I've had diabetes for so long that it's just part of life.'

Talking about diabetes

Most people with diabetes agree that it's best to be open and honest about it with friends and workmates. Many people know very little about diabetes, and may have all sorts of wrong ideas about what it involves and what an affected person can and can't do. The more they know, the more likely they are to accept diabetes in a matter-of-fact way. It's also helpful if they understand about hypos, and know how to help if necessary.

Sports and exercise

Regular exercise is good for everyone, and people with diabetes are no exception. In fact, doctors recommend that exercise should be a central part of the diabetes care plan. Thirty minutes of moderate activity 3-5 times a week is the recommended level. 'Moderate' means exercise that leaves you warm and slightly out of breath, but not panting. However, any physical activity is better than none.

Exercise has the following benefits:

- It reduces the risk of heart disease by helping to keep the heart and circulation healthy, bringing down cholesterol levels and lowering the blood pressure.
- It helps weight control.
- It can improve glucose control.
- It helps you deal with stress.
- It makes you feel better mentally and physically.

Exercise doesn't have to mean playing sport or going to the gym. Walking to work or school, using the stairs instead of the lift or riding an exercise bike in your living room all count, and so does hitting the dance floor to your favourite music!

Basic exercise
Using the stairs is exercise that fits into everyday life.

Exercise and glucose levels

The relationship between exercise and blood glucose is quite complicated, and people with diabetes have to learn to adjust their food intake and medication (especially insulin) to cope with extra physical activity. When the muscles exercise, they burn up extra glucose. To help them get the fuel they need, hormones released during exercise make the body more sensitive to insulin. To prevent a hypo, a person with diabetes will probably need either less insulin or more food, or both. An extra snack may be needed before, during or after exercise. The effect can continue for as long as a day afterwards as the muscles replenish their carbohydrate store. On the other hand, exercise tells the liver to release more glucose into the blood, and this can sometimes cause levels to go too high. Blood testing before and after exercise will reveal what is happening.

Half-time break

A snack during a match is often a good idea, whether you have diabetes or not.

Smoking

Everyone knows that smoking is one of the best ways to damage your health. Not only does it cause cancer, it greatly increases your chances of suffering a heart attack or stroke. As we saw in Chapter 5, the risk of these last two is already higher if you have diabetes. If you smoke as well, the two risks work together. In addition, smoking restricts the flow of blood through the small blood vessels, which are also damaged by high glucose levels in diabetes. Smoking therefore increases the likelihood of developing the long-term complications of diabetes, especially kidney disease and foot ulcers. All in all, smoking and diabetes are a very bad combination.

Sports

Having diabetes doesn't mean giving up competitive sports. People with the condition have been highly successful in many sports: for example, Gary Mabbutt played soccer for England, Wasim Akram captained Pakistan at cricket and rower Stephen Redgrave is the only person ever to win a gold medal at five successive Olympic games.

Feelings about diabetes

Being told you have a disease like diabetes is not easy. You might feel frightened and confused. You might be angry that it has happened to you, or feel guilty and blame yourself, even though it's not your fault. Some people refuse to think about it, and convince themselves (wrongly) that nothing has changed. All these reactions are common and understandable.

Five times gold
Rower Stephen Redgrave has diabetes, but it did not stop him from winning five Olympic gold medals.

'I never want to see a needle or a finger-prick again. Why do I have to go through this when my friends don't? Some days I just can't be bothered with any of it. Who cares if my glucose goes a bit high?'
(Stephanie, 16)

Even people who have had diabetes for a while can have days when they feel down about it. Diabetes is for life and it has to be dealt with every day. Sometimes it can seem just too much to cope with on top of everything else – especially all the usual problems and hassles of growing up. These feelings are natural. If they don't go away, talking to someone who understands diabetes can help. Useful addresses are given on page 62. Diabetes organizations also run groups and holidays especially for young people, so that they can meet others who face the same challenges.

> 'The hardest thing about diabetes is having to think about it every day, and knowing that it's for the rest of your life. You learn to deal with it, but I do get angry about it sometimes.' (Sylvia, hairdresser)

Holiday
An adventure holiday builds confidence in many ways.

It's my life ...

To a large extent, it's up to the person concerned how much diabetes affects their life. We know that good glucose control – keeping blood glucose as close to normal levels as possible – greatly reduces the chances of long-term complications over the years. Once someone knows the facts, it's up to them how much commitment they want to put in to their diabetes care. Some people take it very seriously while others decide to put up with higher glucose levels in return for a more relaxed attitude to their diet and lifestyle. The diabetes care team is there to help people think through the issues and come up with solutions that they can live with.

'Doctors and diabetes teams are constantly amazed at how well the vast majority of people with diabetes cope, and how quickly they adapt to the demands of treatment and management.'
(Dr Dick Shillitoe, clinical psychologist)

Diabetes (mainly type 2) will affect more and more people unless the trend towards obesity and lack of exercise is reversed. However, improved knowledge and better treatment mean that people diagnosed with the condition can expect a longer, healthier life than ever before. New methods of insulin delivery and blood monitoring are likely to make coping with the disease easier. There is also a real possibility of finding a cure for one or both types of diabetes – perhaps by the time today's affected children grow up.

Research
Researchers may find a cure for diabetes, within the lifetime of young people reading this book.

Sorted about diabetes!

Helen developed diabetes when she was 13. Now 17, she feels she has learned a lot since then.

'At first it was really frightening. The doctor was talking about blood tests and injections and I felt I couldn't possibly cope with it all. But it wasn't long before I was managing fine.

After a year or so I went through a phase of really hating diabetes. I wanted to start going out more, but I felt my parents weren't giving me enough freedom because of my diabetes. We had a lot of rows.

Then someone suggested a diabetes summer camp. Meeting other people who were going through the same thing was a real help; my friends are great but they can't really understand what diabetes is like because they haven't got it. My parents also realized that I could take care of myself, so they started letting me do more on my own.

I'm quite good about taking care of myself, but I'm not perfect. Who is? I've done a few things that, looking back, weren't a great idea. Now I realize that the more sorted I am about diabetes stuff, the easier it is to get on with the rest of my life.'

Glossary

abdomen   the region of the body below the chest, containing the stomach and intestines.

amputation   surgical removal of all or part of a limb.

artery   blood vessel that carries oxygenated blood from the heart to the tissues. Veins carry blood back to the heart.

blood glucose   the concentration of glucose in the blood.

blood vessel   an artery, vein or capillary. Capillaries are the tiny vessels that reach every part of our body tissues.

carbohydrates   a group of nutrients made from carbon, hydrogen and oxygen atoms, i.e. sugars, starches and dietary fibre.

chiropodist   a person qualified in treating and preventing foot problems.

cholesterol   a fatty substance found in all cells. It is made in the liver and also contained in foods of animal origin. Too much cholesterol in the blood is linked to heart disease.

coma   prolonged, deep unconsciousness.

complications   health problems that develop over time as a result of diabetes.

constipation   difficulty in passing solid waste.

developed world   the richer, more economically developed countries.

developing world   the poorer, less economically developed countries.

diagnosis   the identification of a disease by a doctor.

dietitian   qualified person who advises on diet, both for treating and preventing diseases.

epidemic   an outbreak of disease affecting many people.

fibre   indigestible carbohydrate, obtained from plant foods (also known as roughage).

gestational   relating to pregnancy.

glucose   the simplest form of sugar, and the end result of carbohydrate digestion.

hormone   chemicals produced at specific locations in the body that regulate the function of cells and organs elsewhere.

hypo   (short for hypoglycaemia); an episode of low blood glucose. Symptoms can include dizziness, shaking, confusion and others.

hypoglycaemia   low blood glucose.

immune system   the system of specialized cells and chemical messengers that protects our bodies from 'foreign' organisms like bacteria.

insulin   a hormone produced in the pancreas that regulates the level of glucose in the blood.

islet cells	the cells in the pancreas that produce insulin.
obesity	being at least 20 per cent above a healthy weight.
pancreas	the organ that makes insulin. Also makes various digestive enzymes.
pathologist	doctor who investigates the causes of disease.
sedentary	describes a lifestyle involving little physical activity.

starch	a complex form of carbohydrate found in plant foods, e.g. potatoes, cereals.
symptoms	the effects felt by a person with a disease or illness, e.g. rash, pain, fever.
ulcer	an open sore.
urination	passing water (peeing).

Resources

Diabetes UK
10 Queen Anne Street,
London W1M 0BD

tel. 020 7462 2791
Careline 020 7636 6112

www.diabetes.org.uk

National organization for people with diabetes. Publishes fact sheets and magazines, raises awareness and funds research. Its website contains useful information on many different aspects of diabetes, and includes a 'Teen zone'.

American Diabetes Association
Customer Service,
1701 North Beauregard Street
Alexandria, VA 22311

tel. 1-800-342-2383 (calls within the USA only)

www.diabetes.org

Provides information and support to people with diabetes and funds research. The website contains the latest news on diabetes and includes a daily recipe.

Diabetes Insight
www.diabetic.org.uk
A UK-based website for people with diabetes.

Children with Diabetes
www.childrenwithdiabetes.com
An online community for children, young people and families affected by diabetes. Based in the USA.

Index